W9-CNA-593

# WARM-WEATHER HOMES

There are about 1,100 species of bats, but only 3 of those species are vampire bats. Most vampire bats belong to the species called common vampire bats. The two other species are hairy-legged vampire bats and white-winged vampire bats.

Vampire bats like warm weather. They live in Central America and South America. They live in deserts and dense rain forests. As people clear forests in South America to make cattle farms, bats move into these areas. To a vampire bat, a herd of cattle is like an all-you-can-eat feast.

Vampire bats, and other bats, often make their homes in caves, the holes of trees, or other cool, dark places. This cave is in South America.

9

# DARK, DRY, AND QUIET

The best home for vampire bats is a place that is dark, dry, and quiet. A cave is just about perfect. Vampire bats also like to live in holes in trees, under rock ledges, and even in buildings. An old church works just as well as a cave for housing vampire bats.

Vampire bats live in **colonies** of from 100 to 2,000 bats. The colonies are made up of females and their young. Males **roost** in a different place. Bats become friends by **grooming** each other. They pick dirt and bugs from each other's fur. Grooming builds strong friendships among bats.

This vampire bat has made its home in a cave. It will leave the cave each night to find food.

# FOLLOW THE HERD

Vampire bats feed on the blood of cattle, sheep, pigs, goats, horses, and, sometimes, even humans. When a vampire bat finds a food source, it cuts open a tiny flap of skin. The bat's **saliva** keeps the animal's blood from **clotting**. The saliva also numbs the area of the cut, so the animal does not feel the bite.

A vampire bat drinks blood equal to more than half of its own body weight. The bat's body can use only red blood cells. Within two minutes of starting to eat, the bat's body rids itself of blood **plasma** in the form of **urine**.

Here a vampire bat feeds on blood from a sleeping cow. Bats will return to the same cow farms over and over to find a sure meal.

# ON THE HUNT

Bats find their food by heat and scent. **Mammals** give off heat when they sleep. Their bodies give off odors, which the bats use to find the animal. They also use **echolocation**. Bats send out a sound. By listening to the **echo**, the bat can figure out how far it is to the food source.

Surprisingly, the bats do not fly to get to their **prey**. Vampire bats are the only bats that move well on the ground. Vampire bats seem to run, much like horses. They get close to the prey, bite, and drink.

Sleeping animals, like these pigs, are a vampire bat's food of choice. If there is fur on the skin, the bat uses its teeth to clip away the fur.

# ENEMIES OF THE VAMPIRE BAT

Bats may be hunters, but they are also prey. Snakes and lizards enter caves where bats roost and attack the sleeping bats. Vampire bats are tiny and do not make much of a meal. To fill up, a lizard would need to eat several bats.

When they fly at night, bats are prey for many birds. Bat hawks, owls, and eagles dive down and catch bats in midair. The bat's most dangerous predator is human, though. Some people fear bats and want to get rid of them. They may even blow up caves to kill the bats.

Owls are excellent hunters. They use their eyes and ears to find prey, then dive down to catch the animal with their feet.

17

# SHARING THE FEAST

Bats must eat every two or three days, or they will die. Bats that have food will share with those that do not. A bat that has a lucky hunt will help feed a friend or relative who was not so lucky.

The hungry bat will beg for food. A bat that has eaten vomits red blood cells to feed its friend. This kindness has a purpose. Today's lucky bat may be tomorrow's hungry bat. Sharing food helps keep all the colony members alive.

This colony of bats lives inside a tree. Bats may live with the same group for over three years and often their whole lives.

19

# THE LIFE OF A VAMPIRE BAT

Bats are mammals, like humans and dogs. Vampire bats produce only one baby a year. A female will carry a baby for six to eight months. Bats do not have births related to the seasons, like birds do. They can give birth at any time during the year.

Baby bats are called pups. After they are born, pups live on their mother's milk. The mother will not hunt for about two weeks after giving birth. During that time, other females feed the mother by sharing their food.

In the wild, vampire bats live about 9 years. In a zoo, they might live for 20 years.

Vampire bat females care for their young for up to nine months. Most other bats care for their young for only three months.

21

# UNDERSTANDING VAMPIRE BATS

Stories make people fear vampire bats. However, it is important to know that vampire bats do not usually bite humans. A vampire bat will not turn into Dracula.

Vampire bats may carry **rabies**, an illness that affects animals and humans. Rabies often results in death. It attacks the nervous system of those who have it.

Scientists think that vampire bat saliva may help with heart attacks and strokes. The saliva is a natural blood thinner, so vampire bats may soon be lifesavers.

# GLOSSARY

**blood vessels** (BLUD VEH-sulz)  Thin tubes, or pipes, in the body through which blood flows.

**clotting** (KLAHT-ing)  Thickening.

**colonies** (KAH-luh-neez)  A group of animals or people living together.

**echo** (EH-koh)  A sound that is bounced back to where the sound originally came from.

**echolocation** (eh-koh-loh-KAY-shun)  Locating an object by emitting sound and following the reflection, or echo, of that sound.

**grooming** (GROOM-ing)  Cleaning the body and making it appear neat.

**mammals** (MA-mulz)  Warm-blooded animals that have a backbone and hair, breathe air, and feed milk to their young.

**plasma** (PLAZ-muh)  The clear, yellowish part of blood.

**prey** (PRAY)  An animal that is hunted by another animal for food.

**rabies** (RAY-beez)  A disease that affects the brain of an animal.

**roost** (ROOST)  To settle or to build a nest.

**saliva** (suh-LY-vuh)  The liquid that forms in the mouth from glands.

**species** (SPEE-sheez)  One kind of living thing.

**urine** (YUR-ihn)  Liquid body waste.

# INDEX

# WEB SITES

Due to the changing nature of Internet links, PowerKids Press has developed an online list of Web sites related to the subject of this book. This site is updated regularly. Please use this link to access the list:
www.powerkidslinks.com/bsu/vbats/